12 TIPS FOR MANAGING
STRESS AND ANXIETY

by Maddie Spalding

www.12StoryLibrary.com

12-Story Library is an imprint of Bookstaves.

Produced for 12-Story Library by Red Line Editorial

Photographs ©: Prasit Rodphan/Shutterstock Images, cover, 1; Volt Collection/Shutterstock Images, 4; Blend Images/Shutterstock Images, 5; Darren Baker/Shutterstock Images, 6; Monkey Business Images/Shutterstock Images, 7; Creatista/Shutterstock Images, 8; Jami Garrison/Shutterstock Images, 9; Brent Hofacker/Shutterstock Images, 10; Nataliya Arzamasova/Shutterstock Images, 11; NAN728/Shutterstock Images, 12; Catalin Petolea/Shutterstock Images, 13, 23; Darrin Henry/Shutterstock Images, 14, 29; djile/Shutterstock Images, 16; Elena Elisseeva/Shutterstock Images, 17, 28; bikeriderlondon/Shutterstock Images, 18; Aschindl/Shutterstock Images, 19; Jaren Jai Wicklund/Shutterstock Images, 20; Soloviova Liudmyla/Shutterstock Images, 21; donatas1205/Shutterstock Images, 22; Pikul Noorod/Shutterstock Images, 24; Uber Images/Shutterstock Images, 25; Rob Marmion/Shutterstock Images, 26

Library of Congress Cataloging-in-Publication Data
Cataloging-in-publication information is on file with the Library of Congress.
978-1-63235-366-5 (hardcover)
978-1-63235-384-9 (paperback)
978-1-62143-508-2 (hosted ebook)

Printed in China

Table of Contents

Practice Positivity 4

Get Moving 6

Talk It Out 8

Limit Caffeine 10

Practice Time Management 12

Look for a Laugh 14

Listen to Calm Music 16

Try Visualization 18

Don't Skimp on Sleep 20

Do Some Light Reading 22

Keep a Journal 24

Stretch the Stress Out 26

Fact Sheet 28

Glossary 30

For More Information 31

Index 32

About the Author 32

Practice Positivity

You walk to the front of the classroom. Your hands shake as you start your speech. Your throat feels dry. Everyone's eyes are on you. You don't know how you're going to get through this.

Have you ever felt this way? If so, you're familiar with anxiety. Anxiety is a worried or nervous feeling. It comes as a reaction to stress. You might start to sweat. You might get a headache. These are anxious reactions to stress.

Anxiety doesn't have only physical symptoms. Anxiety can affect your mind as well. Stress can lead to anxious thoughts. You might start to think, "I'll never get this done."

So, how can you manage anxiety? The first step is to resist negative thoughts. Remind yourself of past situations you got through. This can be a confidence booster. Repeating a comforting phrase can help too. For example, you might

Many people suffer from anxiety when they have to speak in front of groups.

21

Percent of Americans who searched "anxiety" or "stress" on the Internet in 2013.

- Anxiety is a reaction to stress.
- Anxiety includes physical symptoms. It also includes negative thoughts.
- Physical symptoms of anxiety can get worse when negative thoughts build.
- Repeating a supportive phrase can help silence negative thoughts.

ANXIETY DISORDERS

Some people have extreme reactions to stress. For instance, a person might have fear that makes it hard to concentrate at school. Or she may have extreme fear in social situations. Fears that regularly interfere with daily life are called anxiety disorders. If you think you have an anxiety disorder, talk to a doctor. Anxiety disorders are treatable if you seek help.

say, "I will get through this." That can help silence your negative thoughts. You might start to believe this phrase the more you repeat it.

Thinking about a time you were successful can help you get through a stressful situation.

Get Moving

Think about what happens when you exercise. Your heart beats faster. You start to sweat. These things also happen when you're anxious. But exercise affects your body and brain in a different way than stress does.

Your brain releases certain chemicals when you're under stress. Some of these chemicals cause a fear response. Your brain also releases stress hormones. Hormones are chemicals that control how cells and organs work. Stress hormones prepare you to fight or flee from the source of your stress. Your muscles tense up. Your body is on high alert.

When you exercise, your brain releases feel-good chemicals. These chemicals are called endorphins. Endorphins improve your mood. They make you feel more relaxed. Exercise forces you to focus on a single task. Focusing on body movements can shift worries to the back of your mind.

Exercise can offset the effects of stress.

Soccer is a great way to get exercise while having fun.

Many types of exercises can have this effect. Walking for as little as 20 minutes can reduce your anxiety. Other common exercises can also reduce anxiety. They include jogging and cycling. Whatever physical activity you choose, your brain and body will feel the benefits.

THINK ABOUT IT

What kinds of exercises help you relax? Explain how you feel after a workout. Does your reaction to exercise match what is described in this chapter?

14

Percent of people who use regular exercise to relieve stress.

- Your brain releases stress hormones when you're anxious.
- Stress hormones make your muscles tense up.
- Exercising can relieve stress tension.
- Your brain also releases chemicals as you exercise. These chemicals make you feel more relaxed.

Talk It Out

Many people talk with friends during lunch. Others talk to teammates during sports. Talking to others can reduce stress.

Stress can cause negative thoughts. You might think you can't do certain tasks. You might start to feel overwhelmed if your anxiety builds. When this happens, seek out friends or family members. These people may give you the extra encouragement you need. Often, they can help reduce your anxiety.

Some people have small friendship circles. It's okay to have a small number of friends. The quality of

Talking with friends can help reduce stress and anxiety.

Playing basketball with a friend can make you feel more relaxed.

friendships is more important than the number. Having at least one close friend can help reduce your stress and anxiety. Maybe you participate often in healthy activities with your friend. Your best friend may also be your teammate on the track team. Or maybe you and your friend share a love of playing music. Doing activities with a friend can give you the support you need to manage your anxiety.

43
Average minutes per day that Americans spend socializing.

- Stress can produce negative thoughts.
- Talking to friends or family members can reduce negative thoughts.
- Friends or family may give encouragement. This can make your anxiety feel more manageable.
- Social activities can make you feel more relaxed.

SOCIAL ANXIETY

Some people have social anxiety. The idea of talking to others may make them feel anxious. So, talking to others may not be a good way for these people to reduce anxiety. Therapists have a treatment called exposure therapy. First, a person is exposed to minor social situations. Then she faces more common social situations. A therapist may coach her on how to manage her anxiety in these situations.

Limit Caffeine

Caffeine is a stimulant. A stimulant is something that gives you energy. Many kids get caffeine through soda. Chocolate is another common source. Caffeine in small doses can have some positive effects. It can boost your mood. It can also give you more energy. But caffeine has negative effects when you're feeling anxious. Consuming even a small amount can increase your anxiety.

When you feel stress, your brain releases adrenaline. This makes you feel more alert. Your heart rate increases. Your muscles tense. Caffeine has a similar effect. It makes your brain release more adrenaline. Many sodas contain high amounts of caffeine and sugar. Sugar also increases your heart rate. This combination can cause a spike in your adrenaline. Too much adrenaline can make it hard to concentrate.

Many foods and drinks can help reduce anxiety. Consider having a cup of milk instead of soda. Milk can help you feel more relaxed. Fish and nuts can

Too much caffeine can make you feel anxious.

70

Percent of soft drinks that contain caffeine.

- Your brain releases adrenaline when you're under stress.
- Caffeine also boosts your adrenaline levels.
- Consuming caffeine when you're anxious can increase your anxiety.
- Some foods and drinks can help reduce your anxiety.

CAFFEINE DEPENDENCE

Many people get too much caffeine. This can lead to caffeine dependence. That is an unhealthy need for caffeine. Consuming 100 milligrams (0.1 grams) of caffeine per day can lead to dependence. But quitting caffeine all at once can cause bad side effects. You might get headaches. You might get angry easily. The best way to treat dependence is to reduce your caffeine intake slowly.

help too. Fish helps lower your adrenaline levels. And nuts help lower stress hormones.

Avocados have vitamins that reduce stress.

5

Practice Time Management

Stress and anxiety can leave you feeling overwhelmed. You may feel less in control during stressful situations. But you can feel more relaxed and in control by practicing time management.

A calendar can help you prioritize your tasks. Maybe you have a paper that's due on the same day as a

math test. Thinking about both of these tasks at once can make you feel anxious. But separating the tasks into small steps can make them feel more manageable. You could plan to write a couple paragraphs of your paper each night. And you could separate your math material into sections. Plan to study

Keeping track of your tasks in a planner is one way to manage your time.

one section per night. Write out each of these steps on your calendar. Estimate how long each task will take. Write out a scheduled time for each task.

It's okay to take breaks once in a while. In fact, brief breaks can help you re-energize. Consider adding breaks into your schedule. Spread out short breaks between tasks. But take note of things that could distract you. Maybe social media often distracts you from your work. The key is to keep to your time limit.

Using a timer can be helpful. You might be more productive if you do different things during each break. You could try taking a walk. You could also listen to relaxing music.

17
Minutes of break time recommended for each 52 minutes spent working.

- Prioritizing your tasks is an important time management skill.
- Breaking tasks into smaller steps can make them more manageable.
- Scheduling short breaks can help you re-energize.
- Writing down time limits can help you stick to your schedule.

Walking is a healthy way to spend a break, and it has the added benefit of reducing anxiety.

Look for a Laugh

Think about a time you felt anxious. You probably didn't feel like laughing. But if you had laughed, you may have reduced your stress and anxiety. Laughter might not be a medicine that doctors would give you. Still, letting out a laugh every once in a while can help you relax.

Laughter can help you feel more relaxed.

Your brain releases endorphins when you laugh. Endorphins improve your mood. Laughter also reduces your levels of stress hormones. Even expecting a laugh can have these stress-relieving effects. You might be headed to a movie theater to see a funny movie. Or you might be preparing to watch a funny TV show with a friend. Just looking forward to a laugh in situations such as these can relieve some stress.

Laughter can also reduce muscle pain. Your muscles tense when you're anxious. So, anxiety can result in muscle soreness over time. But relaxing your muscles can reduce some of this pain. Laughter also has the positive effects of deep-breathing exercises. You breathe deeply when you laugh. This increases your oxygen intake. It improves your blood flow. These effects will leave you feeling more relaxed.

1998

Year that World Laughter Day, an event promoting world peace through laughter, was founded.

- Your brain releases endorphins when you laugh.
- Laughter reduces your levels of stress hormones.
- Laughing reduces muscle tension. This makes you feel more relaxed.
- Laughter distracts you from the source of your stress.

Laughter also distracts you. For a while, you won't think about the source of your stress. Focusing all your attention on the source of your stress can leave you feeling exhausted. So, consider taking a break to focus on something that makes you laugh. It can re-energize your brain. And that can help relieve some of your anxiety!

15

Listen to Calm Music

A certain song might remind you of when you first heard it. A song may also bring back emotions linked with that memory. Music can have a calming effect when it's linked with a happy memory. But music that isn't linked to any memories can also have a calming effect. Soft and melodic music can be soothing. This could include classical music or jazz. Every person has his or her own preferences.

Some psychologists use music to treat people. This method is called music therapy. It can be helpful for people who have anxiety disorders. Listening to calm music

Listening to calm music can relax your muscles.

MUSIC THERAPY FOR VETERANS

Music therapy first became popular after World War II. Many soldiers had post-traumatic stress disorder (PTSD). They sometimes heard sounds that brought back memories of the war. This made them anxious. Volunteer musicians played calm music to veterans in hospitals. This method helped reduce their anxiety.

66

Percent of US teenagers who listen to music every day.

- Music is linked to emotions and memory.
- Certain kinds of music can have a calming effect.
- Some psychologists use music therapy to treat people.
- Listening to calm music lowers your levels of stress hormones.

THINK ABOUT IT

Do you have music that helps you relax? If so, what kinds of music are on your playlist? If not, think about songs you would put on this playlist.

can lower anxiety. You can try this on your own. Think of some songs that make you feel relaxed. Listen to them whenever you're feeling stressed or anxious.

Listening to calm music lowers your levels of stress hormones. It lowers your heart rate. Your brain releases a feel-good chemical called dopamine when you listen to calm music. All of these changes will leave you feeling more relaxed.

Songs linked to happy memories can help you get through a stressful time.

17

Try Visualization

Have you ever imagined yourself reaching a goal? Maybe you visualized yourself winning a game. Maybe you visualized yourself doing well on a test. This technique can make goals seem more manageable. Practicing visualization can lower your anxiety. It can also make you feel better about your ability.

First, visualize a good outcome. Imagine yourself reaching your goal. Fill in as many details as possible. Think about the sounds and smells. The more realistic your visualization is, the more motivated you'll be to make it happen.

Other kinds of visualization can be helpful, too. Think about a place where you feel calm and relaxed. Close your eyes. Take a few deep breaths. Imagine yourself in that place. Again, fill in the details. Sound recordings can help. Suppose

When you visualize yourself reaching a goal, you may feel more motivated to achieve it.

Visualizing a peaceful cabin in the mountains is one way to feel more relaxed.

you're imagining yourself on a beach. You might play a recording of waves. When all the details are in place, try holding on to your visualization for a few minutes. Let yourself stay in that calm place. Soon, you will feel more relaxed.

6

Number of psychologists on the US Olympic Committee who train athletes in visualization.

- Visualization can make goals seem more achievable.
- Visualizing yourself in a peaceful place can reduce anxiety.
- Fill in details to make your visualizations realistic.
- Visualize until you feel yourself become more relaxed.

BUDDHISM AND MEDITATION

Buddhist monks have a special way of dealing with stress. They meditate. This helps them become calm. They often visualize Buddhist gods and symbols. Meditation is a daily routine for Buddhist monks. Scientists have looked at monks' brain activity while they meditate. These studies have helped experts learn more about brain activity during states of relaxation.

19

Don't Skimp on Sleep

Everyone needs sleep. It helps you recharge at the end of the day. It helps your body and brain recover from stress. Not getting enough sleep can make you feel anxious the next day. But sleep might be difficult when you're anxious at bedtime. Luckily, there are methods that can help you put yourself to sleep.

Try doing a calming activity before bedtime. This could include reading or listening to music. You might also try relaxation techniques. Deep breathing can lower your heart rate. Progressive relaxation is another option. Flex and relax each of your muscles in turn. This will help your body feel more relaxed.

Reading is one way to calm yourself before going to sleep.

If you exercise in the evening, do it at least three hours before bedtime.

Exercising too close to bedtime can make it difficult to fall asleep. Also, try to avoid caffeine four to six hours before bedtime. Avoid using electronics before bedtime, too. Electronic screens give off a certain kind of light. This light makes it harder to get to sleep.

You can also write a to-do list. Make a list of everything that's worrying you. Then put this list in a different room. Keeping this list out of sight might help you put your worries out of your mind.

9

Minimum hours of sleep each night recommended for children aged 6 to 13.

- Sleep helps your brain and body recover from stress.
- Feeling anxious at bedtime can make it difficult to fall asleep.
- Calming activities such as reading can help you fall asleep.
- Avoid exercise and electronics before bedtime.

THINK ABOUT IT

Do you have a bedtime ritual that helps you get to sleep? If so, what do you do? Use the information from this chapter to explain why your current bedtime routine works or doesn't work.

10

Do Some Light Reading

Reading has many benefits. It can make you smarter. It can exercise your imagination. It can expand your vocabulary. Reading can also reduce stress and anxiety.

Think about what you read on a normal day. You probably spend some time reading textbooks. This kind of reading might make you feel stressed. That's because it is associated with school and homework. You might read news stories, too. This material keeps you updated on what's happening in the world. But it can also be stressful. Some stories may be sad or distressing. Consider taking time out of your day to read something fun.

Reading books for fun can help reduce your stress level.

This can help reduce your anxiety after a stressful day.

Pick out reading material on your favorite subjects. Maybe you enjoy fantasy books. Maybe you prefer to read magazines. Set aside some time for quiet reading. This can be a pre-bedtime activity. It will relax your mind. And that will prepare you for sleep.

Reading can reduce stress quickly. Reading distracts you from your daily worries. It lowers your heart rate. It can also relieve muscle tension. Try to do some light reading for at least six minutes each night. That can be enough to reduce anxiety after a long day.

By avoiding textbooks right before bed, you will feel less stressed about schoolwork.

70
Percent of middle school students who read more than 10 books a year.

- Pick out reading material on your favorite subject.
- Set aside time at the end of the day to do some light reading.
- Light reading reduces your stress level.
- Light reading for as little as six minutes each night is enough to reduce anxiety.

Keep a Journal

Think about the kinds of writing you do every day. You might write a school paper. Maybe you write for your school's newspaper. Another type of writing is journaling. Writing regularly in a journal is a good habit to keep. It can reduce stress and anxiety.

Journaling can help you think through your problems. Putting your stress into words can make the problems easier to handle. Journaling might also help you consider problems from a new angle. You may realize that tasks you thought were overwhelming seem more manageable. Organizing your thoughts can be very helpful. You can better understand the source of your anxiety.

Does your anxiety produce negative thoughts? Try writing your negative thoughts on a sheet of paper. Then put the paper in a recycling bin. Getting rid of the written thoughts could make it easier for you to put

Try to set aside a few minutes each day to write down your problems.

them out of your mind. Another idea is to draw a line down the middle of a piece of paper. On the left side, list the sources of stress you're able to change. On the right, list the sources of stress you're not able to change. For example, maybe you can solve an argument you're having with a friend. But you probably won't be able to get out of a math test. It's helpful to understand what you can change and what you can't. This is an important step toward reducing your anxiety.

6

Average number of minutes a US high school student spends on non-homework writing on a weekday.

- Journaling can help you define your stress.
- Journaling can help you consider your problems from a new angle.
- Organizing your thoughts as you journal can help you better understand the source of your anxiety.
- Journaling exercises can help reduce your stress and anxiety.

Your journal can be written in a notebook or typed on a computer.

Stretch the Stress Out

Stress and anxiety can have physical effects. Your muscles may tense. They may start to feel sore if you're under stress for a long period of time. One easy way to reduce stress is to stretch your sore muscles.

Yoga is one of the many ways you can stretch to relieve stress.

20 million

Number of people in the United States who practice yoga.

- Your muscles may tense when you are under stress.
- Your muscles may feel sore if you're under stress for a long period of time.
- Stretching exercises can reduce stress.
- Yoga is a good way to stretch your muscles and reduce stress.

Find a comfortable place to stretch. Then think about which muscles are stiff. You might have a sore neck. Neck pain is one of the most common symptoms of stress. You can easily stretch your neck by tilting your head. Tilting your head to the left will stretch the right side of your neck. Tilting your head to the right will stretch the left side of your neck. If the back of your neck is stiff, try sitting up straight. You can also stand with your knees slightly bent. Drop your chin to your chest. Place your hands on the back of your head. Gently push down with your hands. You will feel a slight stretch in the back of your neck. Try to hold this stretch for 20 to 30 seconds. Doing these stretches can help relieve some of your neck pain.

Muscles in your shoulders, back, and legs might also be stiff from stress. To stretch your shoulder, cross your arm over your chest and apply slight pressure to the shoulder. A simple toe-touching exercise can help you stretch your legs. There are many stretches you could try for your back. You might try lying on your back with your knees bent, then pulling each knee up to your chest. For more complicated stretches, you could try yoga. Yoga includes both stretching and deep-breathing exercises. This makes it a great stress-relieving activity.

Fact Sheet

- One stress hormone the brain releases is called cortisol. Cortisol travels to nearly every part of the body, including hair. In a recent study, archaeologists measured the levels of cortisol in ancient people's hair. They found that ancient people from Peru and Egypt had high levels of cortisol in their hair. This study suggests that some people who lived thousands of years ago experienced extreme stress.

- Feeling anxious before you sleep may disturb your REM (rapid eye movement) sleep. REM sleep is one of the two main stages of sleep. Dreaming happens during REM sleep. Certain brain cells send out P-waves during REM sleep. P-waves help control fear and anxiety while you sleep so that you wake up with less anxiety in the morning.

- There are many different kinds of yoga. One kind of yoga is called laughter yoga. Laughter yoga is based on the principle that laughter can be relaxing. It combines guided laughter with deep breathing exercises.

- Some people use herbal remedies to deal with anxiety. Herbal remedies involve smelling or consuming certain herbs. Some people find herbal remedies to be effective. But there have not been many studies on the effectiveness of herbal remedies.

The use of herbal remedies dates back nearly 3,000 years. People in ancient India and China used herbs to treat physical illness as well as anxiety. Some of these herbs included ginger root and cinnamon.

Glossary

adrenaline
A chemical produced by your body when you are excited, frightened, or angry.

anxiety
A feeling of worry or fear in response to stress.

disorder
A physical or mental illness.

endorphin
A chemical created by the brain that reduces pain.

hormone
A chemical that controls how cells and organs work.

stimulant
A substance that causes an increase in energy.

stress
Worry, strain, or pressure. Stress is a response to a perceived threat.

tension
Tightness or stiffness.

therapy
A treatment for an illness, an injury, or a disability.

For More Information

Books

Moss, Wendy and Robin A. DeLuca-Acconi. *School Made Easier: A Kid's Guide to Study Strategies and Anxiety-Busting Tools.* Washington, DC: Magination Press, 2014.

Schwartz, Heather E. *Stress Less: Your Guide to Managing Stress.* Mankato, MN: Capstone, 2012.

Wroble, Lisa A. *Dealing with Stress: A How-To Guide.* Berkeley Heights, NJ: Enslow, 2012.

Visit 12StoryLibrary.com

Scan the code or use your school's login at **12StoryLibrary.com** for recent updates about this topic and a full digital version of this book. Enjoy free access to:

- Digital ebook
- Breaking news updates
- Live content feeds
- Videos, interactive maps, and graphics
- Additional web resources

Note to educators: Visit 12StoryLibrary.com/register to sign up for free premium website access. Enjoy live content plus a full digital version of every 12-Story Library book you own for every student at your school.

Index

adrenaline, 10–11
anxiety disorders, 5, 16
anxious thoughts, 4

blood flow, 15
breaks, 13, 15

caffeine, 10–11, 21

deep-breathing
    exercises, 15, 20, 27
dependence, 11
dopamine, 17

electronics, 21
endorphins, 6, 15
exercise, 6–7, 15, 21,
    27

friends, 8–9, 15, 25

headache, 4, 11
heart rate, 10, 17, 20,
    23
hormones, 6, 11, 15, 17

journaling, 24

laughter, 14, 15

meditation, 19
muscles, 6, 10, 15, 20,
    23, 26–27
music, 9, 13, 16–17, 20
music therapy, 16

negative thoughts, 4–5,
    8, 24

post-traumatic stress
    disorder, 16
progressive relaxation,
    20
psychologist, 16

reading, 20, 22–23

sleep, 20–21, 23
social anxiety, 9
social media, 13
stretching, 26–27
sugar, 10

talking, 5, 8–9
therapist, 9
time management, 12

visualization, 18–19

yoga, 27

About the Author

Maddie Spalding is an enthusiastic writer and reader. She lives in Minneapolis, Minnesota. Her favorite part of writing is learning about new and interesting subjects.

READ MORE FROM 12-STORY LIBRARY

Every 12-Story Library book is available in many formats. For more information, visit 12StoryLibrary.com.